GREAT ARTISTS

CLAUDE
MONET

Roberto Carvalho de Magalhães

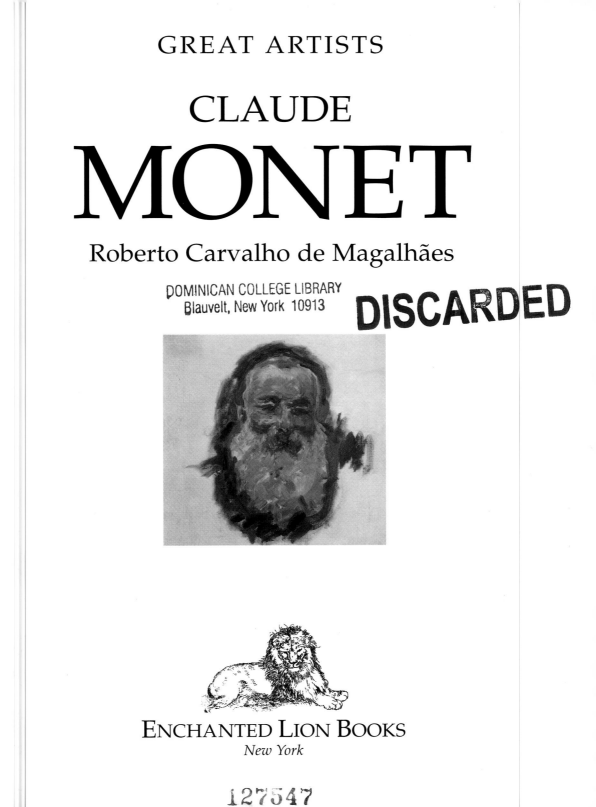

ENCHANTED LION BOOKS
New York

1867 Monet and his first love, Camille Doncieux, have a son, named Jean.

– Frédéric Bazille buys Monet's large painting *Women in the garden,* as a way of giving much-needed financial support to his friend.

– Edouard Manet organizes a solo exhibition at the Champs-du-Mars, to coincide with the *Exposition Universelle.*

COMPLEMENTARY COLORS

The phenomenon of colored shadows had been observed by Goethe in his theory of color (1808–1810). This theory was elaborated by M. E. Chevreul, a chemist at the Gobelins factory. Chevreul noticed that the shadow of an object gave the optical impression of a color opposite, or complementary to, the object itself. The shadow made by the yellow of sunlight, for example, appears tinged with blue. In nature, this phenomenon is fleeting.

Claude Oscar Monet

Claude Monet was born in Paris in 1840. When he was 5 years old his family moved to Le Havre, a thriving port in Normandy, and it was here that Monet grew up. The drawing master at school was Francois-Charles Ochard, a disciple of the great neo-classical painter Jean-Louis David. Ochard taught Monet the rudiments of drawing. At about 15, Monet became well known in the town

for his caricatures of local people, which he sold through an artists' supplies shop for 20 francs each. His sketches were spotted in 1858 by the artist Eugène Boudin, best known for his seascapes. Boudin invited Monet to paint with him on the coast and in the countryside. This period of painting outdoors (*en plein air*) had a profound effect on Monet. Despite his best efforts, he found he was unsuited to learning the academic conventions of painting in the Paris art studios, which seemed dark and restrictive after his time spent painting outdoors. Monet wanted direct contact with the natural world, with its fleeting moments of light and color, and constantly changing moods. More than anything, he wanted to capture his impressions of nature on canvas. Together with Renoir and a few other like-minded painters, he invented a new pictorial language, later termed 'Impressionism.' The Impressionists painted directly in color, usually without preparatory drawings, using

rapid, short brushstrokes. The works shown in this book represent the most significant stages in Monet's long and extraordinary artistic life. In the beautiful winter landscape called *The Magpie*, painted near Etretat in Normandy, Monet makes tangible the phenomenon of colored shadows. The snowy landscape is drenched in winter sunlight, which casts long, blue-violet shadows across the ground. Some research into the scientific theories of color had already been done earlier in the 19th century, and Monet's work now gave it substance. In *The Magpie*, he is not interested in depicting the precise details of the trees or gate, with its magpie; these are rendered only sketchily. It is the intensity of the light — unprecedented in paintings of the time — that he strives to capture, using short brushstrokes of color. The painting evokes not just the look but the sensation of a bright, cold, winter morning.

The Magpie
1868–1869,
oil on canvas,
35 x 51 in.
(89 x 130 cm)
Paris, Musée d'Orsay

1868 Monet's work is admired by Joachim Gaudibert, a businessman from Le Havre. Gaudibert commissions Monet to paint a portrait of his wife.

1869 Monet submits two paintings (one is *The magpie*) to the Salon – France's annual exhibition of 'official' art; both works are rejected.

1870 On June 18, Monet marries Camille Doncieux.

– On July 19, France declares war on Prussia. Monet and Camille move to London, so Monet can escape military call-up. They are joined by Camille Pissarro. Monet meets the art dealer Paul Durand-Reul, a future patron.

– Fréderic Bazille is killed at the front.

Bathers at la Grenouillère

Monet painted this picture on the banks of the Seine, just a few miles from Paris, at the popular floating café, La Grenouillère. People from Paris flocked there by train to spend relaxing weekends bathing, boating, and chatting with friends. Monet and Renoir visited the place together to capture the scene on canvas. Their technique of rapidly applying 'blobs' of color using short, broad brushstrokes was particularly well suited to capturing fleeting reflections of light on gently rippling water, and suggesting the quick movements of animated groups of people.

This detail shows the new technique of painting in 'blobs' of color, used by Monet and Renoir. Here it is used to evoke the movement of water, and broken reflections on the surface. Before long, the Impressionists were using this technique to cover the whole canvas.

Bathers at la Grenouillère
1869, oil on canvas,
29^1/$_4$ x 50^1/$_2$ in. (74.6 x 99.7 cm)
New York, Metropolitan Museum

IN THESE YEARS

1871 The Franco-Prussian war ends. Monet returns to France, via Holland.

He submits no more pictures to the Salon.
1872 Paul Durand-Ruel buys a number of paintings by Monet.

The Thames below Westminster

Monet stayed in London for the duration of the Franco-Prussian war, which lasted a year. While there, he painted a number of works that were influenced by Turner, including this view of the Thames river and Houses of Parliament. In the foreground, a landing stage and several people are silhouetted against the light. Behind them looms Big Ben and the Houses of Parliament, insubstantial and shrouded in fog. River and sky are separated by the low arches of Westminster bridge. Although the reflections in the water beneath the landing stage are reminiscent of *La Grenouillère, The Thames below Westminster* introduces a new dimension to Monet's painting:

diffused light. Here, it filters through the fog that shrouds the buildings, making them appear ghostly and immaterial. Monet's subject is the light itself, and how it influences the way we see things.

The Thames below Westminster
1871, oil on canvas,
18^1/$_4$ x 28^1/$_4$ in.
(47 x 72.5 cm)
London, National Gallery.

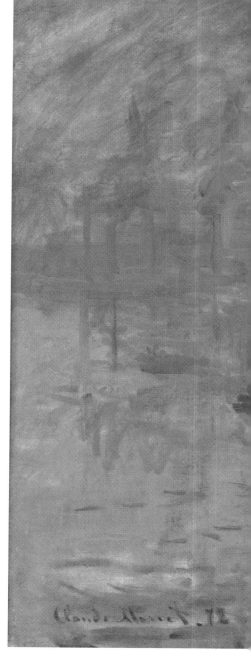

IMPRESSIONISM

It was Monet's 'impression' of the rising sun in this painting that gave rise to the term Impressionism. The critic Louis Leroy saw the painting at the Impressionists first exhibition, and on April 25, 1874, he published an article in the magazine *Charivari* that coined the term 'impression' and poured scorn on the group of rebellious young painters and their 'unfinished' style. The painters themselves sometimes adopted the term 'Impressionist,' but never used it officially. Pissarro preferred to describe the group as 'intransigents,' while Degas chose 'independents.'

Impression: Sunrise

This remarkable painting is of the Seine estuary at Le Havre, at dawn. In style it is reminiscent of *The Thames below Westminster* – diffused light fills the canvas, obscuring all details of the port in the background. But unlike the other painting, here the sun breaks through the morning mist in a bright orange disc and casts broken reflections on the water. The small boat, silhouetted against the light, provides a focal point. At this stage in Monet's artistic development, it is increasingly important for him to evoke poetic content as well as physical atmosphere in his compositions. The picture was one of those exhibited by Monet at the first Impressionist exhibition of 1874.

IN THESE YEARS

1873 Tired of having their works rejected by the Salon, Monet, Renoir, Pissarro and others found the *Anonymous Society of Painters, Sculptors and Engravers* so they can exhibit their paintings independently.

1874 The *Anonymous Society* holds the first Impressionist exhibition. Monet exhibits 12 works.

Edouard Manet declines the invitation to participate. The group breaks up at the end of the year.
– Manet and Renoir

spend some days at Argenteuil; the Monet family features in the paintings they do while they are there.

The Poppies at Argenteuil

In 1872, Monet and his family settled at Argenteuil, a popular weekend boating resort on the Seine to the northwest of Paris. There, Monet painted exclusively out of doors, in direct contact with his subjects: the river alive with sailing boats, the countryside, the road and railway bridges, and the slowly changing seasons. *The Poppies at Argenteuil* belongs to this happy period of the artist's life, during which he perfected his technique of applying small brushstrokes of color. The 'unfinished' appearance of the bright red poppies imbues the scene with a sense of movement and life. At this stage, Monet still often included human figures in his paintings. The reason,

according to Émile Zola, was that Monet, "being a real Parisian brought Paris with him to the country. He could not paint a landscape without the addition of beautifully dressed ladies and gentlemen." Later, Monet dispensed with figures almost completely, so that he could concentrate exclusively on capturing fleeting impressions of nature.

The Poppies at Argenteuil
1873, oil on canvas,
19¹/₂ x 25¹/₂ in.
(50 x 65 cm)
Paris, Musée d'Orsay

Monet's wife Camille and son Jean were the models for the woman and child in the foreground, and probably also for the two figures strolling along the ridge of the hill, to the left of the canvas.

It is often said that spatial depth – or at least linear perspective (used since the Renaissance to ensure a coherent rendering of spatial depth) – disappeared with the Impressionists. But this was not the case. In all Monet's paintings of the road and rail bridges at Argenteuil, not only does the artist observe the rules of linear perspective, but he also ensures that the spatial arrangements of the compositions have appropriate depth.

Monet did 11 paintings of the bridges at Argenteuil: seven of the road bridge (as seen here), and four of the railway bridge.

The Bridge at Argenteuil

While at Argenteuil, Monet developed a new style of brushstroke technique: he reduced the size of the dabs of color and spread them over almost the entire canvas. Water, sky, trees, and boats are all rendered in this way, and the overall effect is one of great luminosity and vibrancy. In this splendid painting, Monet's fascination with

colored shadows reappears – the top part of the bridge, above the arches, is rendered in blue and purple.

The Bridge at Argenteuil, 1874
oil on canvas, 23³/₄ x
31¹/₄ in. (60.5 x 80 cm)
Paris, Musée d'Orsay

1875 Camille Monet falls ill – the start of a long illness. Once again in financial difficulty, Monet is forced to move into a smaller house.

— Two artists influential to the Impressionists die: Camille Corot and Jean-François Millet.

— To combat financial problems, Renoir and Sisley organize an auction of their works. The auction, held on March 24, is a dismal failure.

Edouard Manet 1874, Claude Monet and his wife in his *Studio Boat*, Munich, Neue Pinakothek

The Studio Boat

In his desire to be ever closer to nature, Monet had a studio-boat built for him at Argenteuil. He used it to travel up and down the river, painting from viewpoints not available on land. The idea for his studio-boat came from Charles Daubigny, who had built a floating studio some 15 years earlier. Ever since 1857, Daubigny (a forerunner of the Impressionists) had made trips up and down the Oise river in his boat, painting the river, its traffic, the banks, and the reflections from his studio-cabin. Monet used his floating studio for decades; on one occasion, he and his family traveled in it all the way to Rouen. The boat provided Monet with the viewpoints for a number of important series of paintings, including the *Poplars* and *Mornings on the Seine*. In *The Studio Boat,* as in

so many of his paintings, Monet conveys the feeling of being submersed in nature.

The Studio Boat
1874, oil on canvas,
19$\frac{1}{2}$ x 25$\frac{1}{4}$ in.
(50 x 64 cm)
*Holland, Krüller-
Müller Museum,
Otterlo*

| IN THESE YEARS | and sells *La Japonaise* for the high price of 2,000 francs. He meets the businessman Ernest Hoschedé, who starts | to collect his work. Monet and Hoschedé's wife Alice become close friends. **1877** The third Impressionist | exhibition is held. **1878** Monet's second son, Michel, is born to Camille. The family move to the little village of Vétheuil, on | the Seine. – The writer Théodore Duret publishes his book about the Impressionists. |

1876 At the second Impressionist exhibition Monet exhibits 18 paintings

La Japonaise (Camille in Japanese Costume)

Monet rarely painted portraits. In his early works he generally included people, but seldom delineated their features, preferring instead to merely suggest a person's form and movements using quick strokes of color. This spectacular, full-length portrait of Camille in Japanese costume is an exception, and demonstrates his extraordinary ability as a portraitist. Inspired by his collection of Japanese prints, Monet here pays tribute to Oriental art — a tradition greatly admired by many of the Impressionists. In the painting he not only includes an array of decorative parchment fans and a rich kimono, but also poses Camille in the stance traditionally adopted by courtesans in Japanese prints. Camille's gentle features and the soft drapery contrast with the aggressive posturing of the Samurai embroidered on her kimono.

Eishi Chobuasai
Young Woman,
nishiki-e print,
Paris, Musée des arts
asiatiques Guimet

La Japonaise
1876, oil on canvas,
91 x 55^1/$_2$ in.
(231.5 x 142 cm)
*Boston, Museum of
Fine Arts*

Claude Monet

1

Saint-Lazare Station

Saint-Lazare was the most splendid railway station in Paris, and it was from here that trains departed for some of the destinations best loved and most frequently painted by the Impressionists: the coast of Normandy, Chatou and Bougival (with nearby La Grenouillière), Rouen, Argenteuil, Vétheuil, Giverny, and two of Pissarro's favorite places: Pontoise and Eragny. Railroads had already been treated as a subject in art by the English painter J.M.W. Turner in his *Rain, Steam, and Speed* of 1844, and later by the Impressionist painter Pissarro in his *Station at Upper Norwood,* in 1871. But in both cases, the choice of a railroad as the subject seems almost accidental. For Monet, though, Saint-Lazare – Paris's magnificent modern station – had great symbolic value; it represented the progress of technology. The strong iron ribs of the building were the embodiment of the new industrial age. Trains were becoming an increasingly

markets opened up their gigantic terraces onto the smoky glass walls and roofs of the station (2).... In the bewildering disappearance of the train cars and engines cluttering the tracks, a large red signal stained the pale day (3)....An express train, stationed alone, with two large furious wheels released a thick plume of black smoke, which rose very slowly straight into the calm air... And he then saw an abundant whiteness extending beyond the bridge that swirled like a feathery snow, vanishing into the air through the iron structure."

important part of everyday life, allowing people to experience the world in a totally new way – one of fast, incessant movement. Moreover, for Monet, Saint-Lazare was filled with the most dramatic atmospheric effects: bright light outside, shadows and filtered light beneath the pitched roof, and luminous clouds of steam billowing from the locomotives as they drew into the station. These were his real subjects. In this masterful treatment of *Saint-Lazare Station* – one of a series of 12 paintings – Monet uses his rapid-brushstroke technique, developed in earlier works to convey light filtering through leaves or reflecting off water. Blue shadows are again used, too, in the clouds of steam. Beyond the station, sunlit buildings glow in warm, vibrant yellows and ochre. The dominant colors of the composition are complementaries – colors that contrast in the most extreme way possible: ochre and yellows on the one hand, blues and violets on the other.

2

3

Saint-Lazare Station
1877, oil on canvas, 29¹/₂ x 39¹/₄ in.(75 x 100 cm)
Paris, Musée d'Orsay

IN THESE YEARS

1879 The Impressionists hold their fourth exhibition.

– Camille Monet dies, September 5.

1881 Monet and Alice Hoschedé set up house together at Poissy, with their respective children.

1882 This time Monet takes part in the Impressionists' exhibition.

1883 Monet and Alice Hoschedé move to Giverny.

– Edouard Manet dies.

1884 Monet begins a successful business relationship with gallery owner Georges Petit.

1886 The eighth and final collective Impressionist exhibition is held: Monet does not exhibit. The great innovation was the *pointilliste* style of Seurat, Signac, and Pissarro.

Cliff at Dieppe

Between 1881 and 1886, Monet frequently stayed on the Normandy coast, painting at Fécamp, Pourville, Varengville, Dieppe, and Etretat. He would set up his easel in all weathers and paint the same scene again and again, capturing it in all kinds of light and in different weather conditions. His subjects were cliff faces, rock formations, and natural arches along the coastline. Monet's intention was not to paint exact likenesses of the scenes before him, but rather to show how changes in light alter the way we perceive the world. During his visits to Normandy, Monet painted no fewer than 180 paintings of the coast, often treating the same subject from a number of view points, or painting them at different times of day. The *Cliff at Dieppe* is one of the paintings he made during this period of experimentation. He uses rough brushstrokes to suggest the harshness of the rock face and the wild vegetation growing above. By contrast, the sea and beach below are rendered more smoothly. They are bathed in a white light that contrasts with the strong colors of the foreground to give a sense of spatial depth. Contrasting "light"

with the solidity of the material world in this way was a new method of showing perspective. Outlines, basic to traditional drawing and painting, have ceased to be important. The image, for Monet, emerges from disconnected brushstrokes and continual, subtle changes of color.

Cliff at Dieppe
1882, oil on canvas,
25³/₄ x 32¹/₃ in.
(66 x 82 cm)
Zurich, Kunsthaus

The Estérel Mountains

Monet did not restrict himself to painting the countryside around Paris and the coastline of Normandy. His continual search for new subjects and colors took him to Brittany and the Cote d'Azure in France; Bordighera and Venice in Italy; Holland; Norway; and repeated visits to London.

From mid January to early May of 1888, Monet stayed at

This map shows many of the places where Monet lived and worked.

Antibes, painting in the warm Mediterranean sunshine. One of the views he chose was of the Gulf of Juan, with a distant view of the imposing Estérel mountains in the background.

The mountains are painted with great topographical accuracy, but as in earlier works, it is the diffused light and its effect on color that are the painter's real interest. As in *Cliff at Dieppe*, Monet uses bright, hazy light in the background to throw into perspective the foreground detail – here, a pine tree – and give a sense of spatial depth.

The Estérel Mountains
1888, oil on canvas,
25$\frac{1}{2}$ x 36$\frac{1}{4}$ in.
(65 x 92 cm)
London, Courtauld Institute Galleries

Grain Stacks: Snow Effect

In 1890, Monet grew tired of his wandering lifestyle, and decided to buy the house at Giverny where he and Alice had lived since 1883. The house was surrounded by wheat fields, which in late summer were dotted with huge haystacks shaped like circular huts. From the summer of 1891 until the following winter, Monet made these the subject of a series of at least 25 paintings. He painted them from a variety of angles and in widely varied weather and light conditions. The series was the first of many to bring Monet public and commercial success. They were a turning point: henceforth he was a prosperous artist.

In this painting from the grain stacks series, Monet again returns to the theme of snow and colored shadows, treated so brilliantly – and differently – in *The Magpie* (1869). Two grain stacks provide the focal point. Lit from behind by the winter sun, their long shadows reach toward the viewer across the snowy ground. The light of the sun is yellow with traces of orange, and the haystacks and their shadows are painted in complementary shades of blue, for contrast.

Grain Stacks: Snow Effect
1891, oil on canvas,
25$\frac{1}{2}$ x 36$\frac{1}{4}$ in. (64.8 x 92.1 cm)
Edinburgh, National
Gallery of Scotland

THE SERIES

The principle that the appearance of an object, or our perception of it, changes according to the conditions under which it is viewed led Monet to execute a number of paintings of the same subject from the same viewpoint, but under varied atmospheric conditions and in different lights. Collectively, many works of a single subject, treated differently, are called a 'series.' This repetitive, experimental approach to painting was also adopted by the Impressionist Camille Pissarro.

Rouen Cathedral: the Portal, Morning Fog

In 1892, Monet set up his easel at the first-storey window of a woman's lingerie store in Rouen, and began to paint the first in a series of about 30 paintings of the cathedral opposite. The following year he returned to Rouen to continue painting canvases of the enormous gothic building, only to find that he was no longer welcome in the shop, as his presence there had caused considerable embarrassment to customers! So Monet moved to the shop next door. *The Portal, Morning Fog* belongs to the group painted in 1893 – though it is dated "94" on the canvas, the year when all the paintings were retouched and signed in Monet's studio at Giverny. In this composition, fog suffused with dawn's early light envelops the building and appears to dissolve the solid stone, giving the whole façade a quivering, impalpable quality, like a reflection in water.

Rouen Cathedral: the Portal, Morning Fog
1893, oil on canvas,
39$\frac{1}{4}$ x 25$\frac{1}{2}$ in. (100 x 65 cm)
Germany, Museum Folkwang, Essen

Georges Clemenceau, French statesman and friend of Monet, commented on the series: "The object, dark in itself, receives all its life from the sun, all the power to create a visual impression. But those luminous waves that envelop it, penetrate it, and make it radiate are perpetually changing, struck by high shafts, bursts, or storms of light. What is the model under that fury of living atoms, through which it appears to us, through which it really exists for us? This is what we should look at now, what should be expressed in painting, what the eye should de-compose and the hand re-compose... Looking at Monet's cathedrals close up they seem to be made of who-knows-what indescribable multicolored walls, fragmented on the canvas in a fit of rage. This savage impulse is undoubtedly the fruit of passion, but also of science." (In *La Justice*, 5/20/1895)

Light and shadow are crucial in defining the shape and form of the cathedral's great rose window. Tones of color give the shadows depth.

Rouen Cathedral: the Portal and Tour d'Albane, Full Sunlight

In this version of Rouen Cathedral – in which the subject is viewed from exactly the same angle as in the previous painting – the ornate façade is more clearly visible and more solid-looking in the strong light of the midday sun. The light plays over the complex solids and voids of the building's surface. The dominant colors are once again complementaries, used for optimum contrast: shades of yellow and violet, orange and blue.

Rouen Cathedral: the Portal and Tour d'Albane, Full Sunlight
1894, oil on canvas
42 x 28½ in. (107 x 73 cm)
Paris, Musée d'Orsay

IN THESE YEARS

1892 Monet is at last able to marry Alice Hoschedé, now that she is a widow.

– Monet's *Poplar* series, exhibited at the Durand-Ruel gallery, enjoys the same public and commercial success

as his earlier *Grain stacks* series.

1893 Paul Gauguin returns from his first stay in Tahiti. (Gauguin's early works

were inspired by the Impressionists, but he later became a leading figure among the Symbolists.)

Morning on the Seine, near Giverny

A small tributary of the river Epte flowed through Monet's land at Giverny and fed his famous water-lily pond. From 1896 to 1897, according to journalist Maurice Guillemot, Monet would leave his house before dawn and take his boat along the river to an island where the Epte flowed into the Seine. There he worked from a studio boat on 14 paintings at the same time. The composition and viewpoint was the same in all of them: the upper half of each canvas was filled with sky, trees, and river bank; the lower half with water and its reflections of the sky and

trees. As in his earlier *Grain Stack* and *Cathedral* series, he again painted the same scene in all kinds of different light and at different times of day. But where the *Morning on the Seine* series differs is in the way Monet conveys a sense of being completely surrounded by his subject, rather than painting it from a distance. In this splendid version of *Morning on the Seine,* a morning mist envelops the scene, obscuring all details. Vivid blues and flashes of other colors are used more than ever to evoke sheer atmosphere, in a work that is almost abstract.

Morning on the Seine, near Giverny
1897, oil on canvas, 35¹/₄ x 36¹/₂ in. (89.9 x 92.7 cm)
USA, North Carolina Museum of Art

Houses of Parliament, Sunset
1904, oil on canvas,
31³/₄ x 36¹/₄ in., (81 x 92 cm)
Paris, Musee d'Orsay

Houses of Parliament, Sunset

Between 1899 and 1901 Monet made three visits to London to paint the Thames river, its bridges and the Houses of Parliament. During his stay he produced some 65 paintings, 19 of which feature the monumental neo-gothic building. His return to London was a tribute to the city that had sheltered him during the Franco-Prussian war. He was also returning to the subject that years earlier had been the inspiration for his individual style, and had allowed him to make breakthroughs in his personal artistic development. In London, he had developed a new pictorial language in art.

In this composition, dense fog swirls across the river in wispy diagonal brushstrokes, and the buildings rise above it in a continuation of vertical blue strokes. Monet's years of experience painting nature shines in the confident brushwork that blends water and sky as one entity. The strong reds and yellows of a fiery sunset burn a hole in the fog and light up the water momentarily, giving the painting an emotional charge as strong, if not stronger, than its atmospheric intensity.

Waterlilies with Weeping Willows

At the end of 1892, Monet bought a swampy piece of land adjoining his property at Giverny, and set to work transforming it into a watergarden. With the help of a team of gardeners, he planted trees and flowers, and created a pond by diverting a small river that ran across his land. In spring, a profusion of waterlilies blossomed on the water. Monet used his painterly skills to design the vistas and choose the colors for the garden; and he made the focal point a Japanese-style bridge across the water.

Monet's first paintings of the watergarden were of the plants reflected in the water. Then, in about 1897, he embarked on a series of paintings of the Japanese bridge. But from 1903 until his death in 1926, Monet made the waterlilies his cental theme: they were a continual source of inspiration to him. In this composition, *Waterlilies with Weeping Willows*, the viewpoint is close to the water's surface. Spatial depth is suggested by the dimensions and details of the leaves. Monet uses horizontal brushstrokes to suggest the rounded leaves of waterlilies floating close to him; these become less defined near the top of the canvas, which gives a sense of a receding plane. He uses wavering diagonals and verticals for the reflections of the more distant willows, and pastel shades for the sky above. Here, and in his later, huge waterlily paintings, he wants to surround the viewer in a spectacle of color.

In his old age, Monet further experimented with the interplay between light and perception in his monumental series of Water Lily paintings that now hang in the oval rooms of the Orangerie in Paris, where the viewer is surrounded by a spectacle of colour and feeling unrivalled in 20th-century painting.

Waterlilies with Weeping Willows
1907, oil on canvas, 41¼ x 28½ in. (105 x 73 cm) Tokyo, Bridgestone Museum of Art.

1903 The death of Camille Pissarro, a charismatic figure in painting of the second half of the nineteenth century, of equal importance to the Impressionists as to their successors.

1904 Monet travels by car with his wife to Madrid but no paintings result from the journey.

1908 Monet has increasing problems with his eyesight, which will culminate in an operation in 1923.

1910 A watercolor by Kandinsky entirely without reference to reality annouces the birth of abstract painting.

1911 Alice Monet dies.

1922 Monet donates the *Waterlillies* series of paintings to the French state.

1926 Monet dies on 5 December in his house at Giverny, at the age of 86.

The Doge's Palace in Venice
1908, oil on canvas,
31³/₄ x 39¹/₃ in. (81 x 100 cm)
New York, Brooklyn Museum.

The Doge's Palace in Venice

Monet was 68 years old when he and his wife Alice stayed in Venice. He wrote to his friend the art critic Gustave Geffroy, "It is a pity I didn't come here when I was younger and more daring!" Deeply impressed by the light, the water reflecting from the canals onto the buildings, and the whole atmosphere of the city, he worked on 37 canvases which he finished in his studio in Giverny. This painting shows the Dogi Palace with the Grand Canal shimmering in the foreground. The painter has focussed his attention on the light, the haziness of the palace in the morning sunlight, and its rippling reflection in the constantly moving waters of the canal. As always, it is the endless movement of the elements and the way this conditions our perception of

the world that interests
Monet most of all.

Index of Monet's works:

* The numbers in bold refer to the pages where the work is reproduced.

First American edition published in 2003 by
Enchanted Lion Books
115 West 18th Street, New York, NY 10011
Copyright © 2002 McRae Books Srl
English language text copyright © 2003 McRae Books Srl
All rights reserved
Printed and bound in the Slovak Republic

Library of Congress Cataloging-in-Publication Data
Magalhaes, Roberto Carvalho de.
    Claude Monet / Roberto Carvalho de Magalhaes.—1st American ed.
    p. cm.— (Great artists)
    Includes index.
    Summary: Discusses the style and technique of the French Impressionist painter
Claude Monet.
    ISBN 1-59270-009-8
    1. Monet, Claude, 1840-1926—Criticism and interpretation—Juvenile literature.
[1. Monet, Claude, 1840-1926. 2. Artists. 3. Painting, French. 4. Art apreciation] I.
Monet, Claude, 1840-1926. II. Title. III. Great artists (Enchanted Lion Books)

ND553.M7M284 2003
759.4—dc21   2003049055

The series "Great Artists" was created and produced by
McRae Books Srl, Borgo Santa Croce, 8, Florence, Italy
Info@mcraebooks.com
Series editor: Roberto Carvalho de Magalhães
Text: Roberto Carvalho de Magalhães
Design: Marco Nardi Layouts: Laura Ottina
The Publishers would like to thank the following museums and archives
who have authorized the reproduction of the works in this book:
The Bridgeman Art Library, London (9, 34); Scala Group, Florence (Cover, 1, 3, 4-5, 6-7, 10, 11, 13, 15, 16-17, 18, 21, 22-23, 24, 25, 26, 27, 28, 29, 30, 31, 33, 35, 37, 39).

Cover: **Impression: Sunrise,** 1872 (detail)
Page 1: **Self-portrait**, c.1917